NEW YORK

in words and pictures

BY DENNIS B. FRADIN

MAPS BY LEN W. MEENTS

Consultant:
Dr. Wendell Tripp
Editorial Associate and
Chief of Library Services at the
New York Historical Association

CHILDRENS PRESS ®
CHICAGO

For my dear aunt, Frances
Fradin Oscodar

For their help, the author thanks:
Jack MacBean, New York Convention and Visitors Bureau
Dr. Edwin Karp, Department of Geology, New York University
Dr. Howard D. Winters, Professor of Anthropology, New York University
Dr. Thomas Neumann, Professor of Anthropology, Syracuse University
Dr. Howard H. Flierl, retired Professor of Geography, State University of New York at Albany

Mount Jo in the Adirondack Mountains

Library of Congress Cataloging in Publication Data

Fradin, Dennis B
    New York in words and pictures.

    SUMMARY: Introduces the history, cities, industries,
tourists sights, and famous people of the state named
after the English Duke of York.
    1. New York (State)—Juvenile literature.
|1. New York (State)| I. Meents, Len W. II. Title.
F119.3.F68   974.7   80-28366
ISBN 0-516-03932-6

    9 10 R 90 89

Picture Acknowledgments:
NEW YORK STATE DEPARTMENT OF COMMERCE—2, 6, 18, 20 (left),
21 (left), 23 (right, top and bottom), 24, 26, 27, 30, 31, 35, 42 (right, top
and bottom)
JAMES P. ROWAN—7, 15, 16, 20 (right), 29, 36, 38, 41, 42 (top left)
WASHINGTON'S HEADQUARTERS STATE HISTORICAL SITE—11
NEW YORK STATE OFFICE OF PARKS AND RECREATION—13, 43
(bottom center)
AMERICAN AIRLINES—cover, 19, 21 (right, top and bottom), 23 (left,
top, middle and bottom), 25, 42 (bottom left)
CORNING GLASS CENTER—32 (left)
EASTMAN KODAK COMPANY—32 (right), 33 (left)
INTERNATIONAL MUSEUM OF PHOTOGRAPHY AT GEORGE EAST-
MAN HOUSE—33 (right)
UNITED STATES POSTAL SERVICE—40
COVER—Aerial view of lower Manhattan

New York

New York is a state in the northeastern United States. It was named after the English Duke of York.

New York is a leader in many ways. It is a top state for producing milk, grapes, and apples. Its factories make it a top manufacturing state. The state also has our country's biggest city—New York City.

Do you know where our country's capital was located when George Washington was elected president? Or where Franklin D. Roosevelt and three other presidents were born? Do you know where the National Baseball Hall of Fame is located? Or where you can see the Statue of Liberty and Niagara Falls?

You'll soon see that the answer to all these questions is—New York, the Empire State!

Long before people lived in New York, animals lived there. Mastodons—which looked like elephants—roamed about. Horses, seals, and giant beavers were there. Fossil remains of these animals have been found.

Over a million years ago the Ice Age began. Huge mountains of ice, called *glaciers,* moved down from the north. The glaciers covered most of New York. In places, the ice may have been a few thousand feet thick. The glaciers deepened valleys. These valleys later filled with water and became lakes. Many of New York's lakes were formed in this way.

People first came to New York over 11,000 years ago. The earliest people were mainly hunters. They hunted deer and other animals. Their stone spear points and tools have been found.

In more recent times, two groups of Indians lived in New York. One was the Iroquois (EAR • ah • kwoi) group. The Mohawk, Oneida (oh • NI • dah), Cayuga (kay • OOH • gah), Onondaga (on • un • DAH • guh), and Seneca (SEN • eh • kah) were the five tribes of this group.

The Algonkian (al • GONG • kee • in) family was the other Indian group. The Mohican (mo • HE • kan), Munsee, and Delaware were three of the Algonkian tribes.

Indian women farmed. They grew corn, beans, squash, and tobacco. The men hunted deer and bears in the forests. The animal meat provided food. The animal skins were used to make clothes and shoes.

The Hudson River, where Verrazano was thought to have sailed

The Algonkian Indians lived in *wigwams*. These were huts made of poles and tree bark. The Iroquois built *long houses*. Several families lived in a long house, which could be up to 200 feet in length.

Some New York Indians gathered shells. They made them into beads, called *wampum*. Wampum was used as money. The Indians also made pottery, snowshoes, and tools that can be seen in New York museums today.

It is not known for sure who first explored New York. Some say it was Giovanni da Verrazano (jo • VAH • nee dah vair • ret • ZAH • no). Verrazano was an Italian sailor and pirate. He is thought to have sailed into New York Bay and then into the Hudson River in about 1524.

Fort Ticonderoga is on Lake Champlain.

In 1609 the French explorer Samuel de Champlain
(sham • PLANE) set out from Canada. With Champlain
were two Frenchmen and some Algonkian Indians.
They paddled their canoes down a big lake. Samuel de
Champlain named it Lake Champlain—for himself.
Champlain and his men met some Iroquois Indians, near
what is now Ticonderoga, New York. The two groups
fought. The Frenchmen had guns. They won this battle.

The explorer Henry Hudson also arrived in 1609.
Hudson was an Englishman. He worked for the Dutch
(people of The Netherlands). Henry Hudson sailed his
ship, the *Half Moon,* up a river in New York. This river
was later named the Hudson River, after him.

7

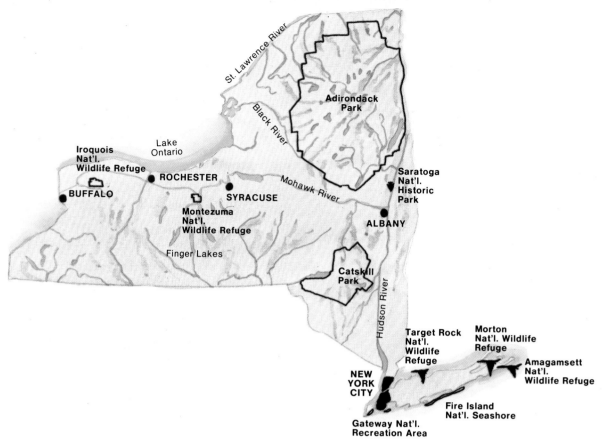

Based on Henry Hudson's trip, The Netherlands claimed a big area. It included parts of what are now New York, New Jersey, Delaware, and Connecticut (keh NET • eh • cut). This area was named *New Netherland*.

Dutchmen traded blankets and liquor to the Indians. In return they received beaver and other animal skins. The skins were worth a lot of money. They were used to make clothes in Europe.

The Dutch also formed settlements. The first was built in 1624 at Fort Orange, which is now the city of Albany.

In 1625 the Dutch began building a town on Manhattan Island. The Indians helped the colonists build huts. The Indians taught the colonists how to hunt and then gave them corn when food ran low.

In 1626 the Dutch leader Peter Minuit (MIN • you • et) bought Manhattan Island from the Indians. The Indians were paid about $24 worth of knives, beads, and farm tools. The Dutch called their settlement *New Amsterdam*. Today, it is New York City.

The Dutch founded other towns in New York. Breuckelen (BROOK • lin), now Brooklyn, and Schenectady (skeh • NECK • teh • dee) were two of them. Rich Dutch people, known as *patroons*, were given grants of large pieces of land.

The English were interested in settling there, too. English people came from Massachusetts (mass • ah • CHEW • sets) and Connecticut. They settled on Long Island. In 1664 the English sent some warships to take control of New Netherland. The Dutch gave the land up without a fight.

The English renamed the land *New York* in honor of the Duke of York. He later became James II, king of England. Under English rule, much of New York was still owned by rich landowners. They owned large pieces of land, called *manors*.

Starting in 1689, England and France fought over lands in America. These wars are often called the French and Indian Wars. Algonkian Indians sided with the French. Iroquois Indians sided with the English. Many bloody battles were fought in New York. The English finally won in 1763.

But soon people in the American colonies talked of freeing themselves from England. They were tired of paying taxes to the English. They no longer wanted to be told what to do by English soldiers, judges, and rulers. In New York and other colonies, the "Sons of Liberty" spoke of forming a new country. They knew they would have to fight a war with England to do it.

Hasbrouck House was used as Washington's Headquarters during the last part of the Revolutionary War.

War between the American colonies and England began in 1775. This was the start of the Revolutionary War. Many New York people were loyal to the king of England. Such people were called *Loyalists*. But the Sons of Liberty and other New York people joined George Washington's army.

New York was the scene of about 92 Revolutionary War battles. Nearly a third of all Revolutionary War battles were fought there.

The Americans under George Washington were beaten in the Battle of Long Island, in 1776. The English then took control of New York City. But the Americans won one of the bloodiest battles of the Revolutionary War in August of 1777. This was the Battle of Oriskany (oh • RISS • keh • nee), fought near what is now the village of Oriskany, New York. Two months later, in October of 1777, the Americans won the Battle of Saratoga, also in New York. After this big battle the English had to surrender an army of about 6,000 men.

By 1783 the Americans had won the Revolutionary War. A new country—the United States of America— had been born.

New York became the eleventh state on July 26, 1788. Kingston was the first state capital. It wasn't until 1797 that Albany became the capital, as it is today.

You probably know that Washington, D.C. is the capital of our country. But from 1785 to 1789 New York City was our nation's capital. It was in New York City in

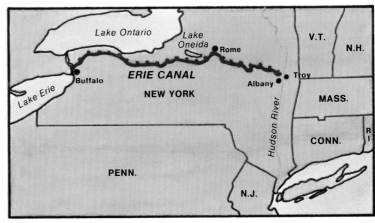

ROUTE OF THE ERIE CANAL

Above: Lock Park at the Erie Canal
Right: A map showing the route of the
    Erie Canal

1789 that George Washington took the oath of office to
become our first president.

In the early 1800s many Americans went to live in
New York. Thousands went to live in New York City. By
1800 New York City was the biggest city in the United
States—as it is today. Other people went to the state to
farm. By 1820 the state had over 1,372,000 people.

New York City factories were making many products.
But it was hard to take those products west over land. In
1825 a boat canal called the Erie Canal was completed
across the state. Boats now took New York City
products to states farther west. Farm products from the
west went by boat to New York City.

In the 1830s and 1840s railroads were built in the state. Products from the Empire State could now go by train to other parts of the country. The Erie Canal and the railroads helped make New York the top manufacturing state by 1850.

New York also produced some interesting people in the 1800s. Martin Van Buren (1782-1862) was born in Kinderhook. He began to study law when he was just 14 years old. Van Buren was elected governor of New York. From 1837 to 1841 he served as our 8th president.

Millard Fillmore (1800-1874) was born in Locke. Fillmore taught school while he studied to become a lawyer. In 1848 Fillmore was elected vice-president. When President Zachary (ZACK • ah • ree) Taylor died, Millard Fillmore became our 13th president. He served from 1850 to 1853.

A statue of John Brown, who helped runaway slaves escape to Canada

While Millard Fillmore was president, Northerners and Southerners argued over slavery. In the South, slaves were used to grow crops. Many Northerners thought that slavery was wrong and wanted to end it.

Some Northerners even helped slaves escape to freedom. A law said that slaves who escaped to Northern states had to be returned. But those who escaped all the way north to Canada were free. Slaves went to Canada on the "Underground Railroad." It wasn't underground. And it wasn't a railroad. The Underground Railroad was a series of houses where slaves hid on their journey to Canada. Some New York people turned their houses into Underground Railroad "stations."

John Brown's Farm, in North Elba, where John Brown is buried

Two famous New York women spoke out against slavery. One was a black woman named Sojourner (so • GERN • er) Truth, who was born in Ulster County. The other was Elizabeth Cady (KAY • dee) Stanton, who was born in Johnstown. Truth and Stanton also worked for the rights of women.

New York people used the printed word to fight slavery, too. In 1847 a black man named Frederick Douglass founded an antislavery newspaper in Rochester. It was called the *North Star*.

Meanwhile, Northerners and Southerners still argued over slavery, taxes, and other issues. The talking ended. In 1861, war between the Northern and Southern states began. This was the Civil War. New York sent more soldiers to fight on the Northern side than any other state. It also provided more supplies than any other state. In 1865 the North won the Civil War.

To people in other countries, the United States was the "Land of Opportunity." During the 1800s and early 1900s, people from many lands came to the United States. Millions entered our country at Ellis Island in New York Harbor. Many of those people made their homes in New York City. New York City was called a *melting pot*. This was because people of many cultures became Americans there.

Just as two New York men were president during the 1800s, two became president during the 1900s. Theodore Roosevelt, born in New York City, was our 26th president from 1901 to 1909. His cousin Franklin Delano Roosevelt was our 32nd president from 1933 to 1945.

While Franklin D. Roosevelt was president, the United States entered World War II. Over 1½ million New York men and women helped the United States and its allies win this war. New York factories produced airplanes and other materials needed for the war effort.

At the end of World War II, the nations of the world saw that they must try to avoid future wars. The countries formed a group in which they worked together for peace. It was called the United Nations. New York City became United Nations (UN) headquarters.

The United Nations headquarters, finished in 1952

Midtown Manhattan and the East River

Today, the Empire State has over 18 million people. Only California has more people. New York City and other big cities make the state a leader for manufacturing. The state is number one for making clothes. It is the top state for publishing books and magazines. It is also a leader for producing milk and many other farm products.

You have learned about some of New York's history. Now it is time for a trip—in words and pictures— through the Empire State.

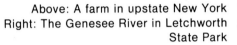
Above: A farm in upstate New York
Right: The Genesee River in Letchworth
State Park

Pretend you're in an airplane high above New York. Below, you can see many kinds of scenery. New York has mountains—such as the Adirondacks (add • eh • RON • dacks). It has many blue lakes and rivers. A huge body of water—the Atlantic Ocean—touches southeastern New York. The state also has forests, farms, and big cities.

Your airplane is landing in one of the world's largest cities. This is New York City. It lies where the Hudson River empties into the Atlantic Ocean. Today New York City has the most people of any city in our country. It is a great center for banking, printing, education, and manufacturing.

Top right: The Brooklyn Bridge
Above: The Verrazano-Narrows Bridge
Bottom right: The Statue of Liberty

New York City is made up of five parts, called
boroughs. The boroughs are: Manhattan, Brooklyn, the
Bronx, Queens, and Staten Island. In places the city's
boroughs are separated from each other by water. The
Brooklyn Bridge, the Verrazano-Narrows Bridge, and
other bridges help you cross the water as you go from
place to place.

To start your New York City visit, take a boat out to
Liberty Island in New York Harbor. The famous Statue
of Liberty can be seen there. This huge statue shows a

21

151-foot-tall woman holding a torch. The Statue of Liberty was given to our country by the people of France, in 1884. It reminds us that the United States was founded as a land of freedom.

Don't get a sore neck looking up at the city's skyscrapers. The Empire State Building, the World Trade Center towers, and the Chrysler Building are just some of New York City's famous skyscrapers.

Even New York City's streets are famous! Wall Street is known for its banks and the New York Stock Exchange. The Broadway area is known for its many theaters.

You'll enjoy the city's many museums. Visit the American Museum of Natural History. There you can learn about dinosaurs and our planet Earth. At the Hayden Planetarium you can learn about stars. The Metropolitan Museum of Art is our country's biggest art museum. At the Museum of Modern Art and the Guggenheim Museum you can enjoy modern art.

22

There are many interesting sights in New York City. Left top: The Empire State Building towers above the others. Left middle: Central Park lies in the center of the city. Left bottom: The twin towers of the World Trade Center are near the Hudson River. Above top: An aerial view showing many of New York's skyscrapers. Above: The George Washington Bridge spans the Hudson River.

Lincoln Center
at night

Do you like music? Go to a concert in Carnegie Hall. At Lincoln Center for the Performing Arts you can enjoy concerts, opera, and ballet.

You'll see many kinds of people in New York City. You'll see a lot of black people. People of Jewish, Italian, Puerto Rican, Irish, German, Chinese, and Polish background also live in the city. Fancy museums and skyscrapers are just one side of the city. Many New York City people live in old, crowded buildings.

The people of New York City work at many jobs. Many make clothes. Others work at producing books and magazines. New York City does more printing than any other U.S. city. The three major TV networks also have their headquarters in the city.

Left: Rockefeller Plaza off Fifth Avenue
Above: Lower Manhattan and the harbor area

Products leave New York City by plane, truck, train, and boat. Ships from all over the world come in and out of the Port of New York. It handles the most cargo of any port in the United States.

You'll see a lot of college students in New York City. New York University, Columbia University, and the City University of New York are just three of the city's schools. About 175,000 students attend the City University of New York.

New York City is also a big sports city. The Yankees and the Mets are the city's major league baseball teams. The Giants and the Jets are the pro football teams. The Knickerbockers are the basketball team. The Rangers and the Islanders are the hockey teams.

Cadets on parade at West Point

About 50 miles north of New York City visit the United States Military Academy at West Point. Officers for the U.S. Army are trained here. The U.S. Military Academy was founded in 1802. It's our country's oldest military college. General Robert E. Lee and presidents Ulysses (you • LISS • eez) S. Grant and Dwight D. Eisenhower are three famous West Point graduates.

From West Point, head about 100 miles north to Albany. Albany is the oldest city in New York and one of the oldest in our country. Dutch settlers built Fort Orange here in 1624. In its early years Albany was a big fur-trading center. Albany has been the capital of the Empire State since 1797.

Visit the State Capitol building in Albany. Lawmakers from all across New York meet here. You can watch them as they work on laws for the Empire State.

Left: New York grows many apples.
Middle: Many ducks are raised on Long Island.
Right: The State Capitol building in Albany

Visit the New York State Museum in Albany. There you can learn about the people, animals, and land of New York. The New York State Museum is the oldest state museum in our country.

New York State has a lot more than big cities. As you travel about, you'll see many farms. You'll see lots of cows. They make New York a top state for producing milk, butter, and cheese. New York is the second leading apple-growing state.

You could eat well if you ate nothing but New York farm products. Beef cattle, hogs, sheep, and chickens are raised in the state. New York chickens produce about two billion eggs a year—enough to make an omelet taller than the Empire State Building!

Lettuce, celery, potatoes, tomatoes, and onions are some of the vegetables grown in New York. The Empire State is a leader for growing pears, cherries, and grapes. The grapes are used to make juice, jam, and wine. Do you like maple syrup on your pancakes? New York is also a top state for producing maple syrup.

You'll enjoy a trip into northeastern New York State. You'll enter the Adirondack Mountains. The state's highest point is in the Adirondacks. It is Mount Marcy, which is 5,344 feet above sea level.

Above: The Ausable River
Left: Adirondack Park

You'll see forests in the Adirondacks—and in many areas of the state. Maple, white pine, ash, spruce, and birch are some of the trees you'll find. In all, about half of New York is wooded.

Many animals enjoy the forests. You can see deer and foxes. Beavers and black bears can also be found. Wild turkeys and pheasants are two of the state's birds.

Skiers in the 1979 World Cup

People also like the forests, mountains, and rivers of New York. In the summer, some people hike and camp in the woods. Others canoe on the state's rivers. In the winter, people ski and snowmobile in the mountains.

Visit Lake Placid in northeastern New York. Glaciers helped form this lovely lake long ago. The 1932 and 1980 winter Olympic Games were held at Lake Placid.

New York has been important in sports history. The early Dutch settlers brought a game called *ninepins* to New York. In 1845 Alexander Cartwright of New York City formed our country's first baseball club. It was called the *Knickerbocker Base Bail Club of New York*.

Left: Children enjoying a ride on
the Erie Canal.
Middle: Visiting the Baseball Hall
of Fame
Above: The Lake Placid area

You'll enjoy a visit to the National Baseball Hall of
Fame in Cooperstown, New York. You can learn about
baseball's greatest players there. You can also learn
about the history of the sport. Cooperstown is where
Abner Doubleday is said to have invented baseball.

Syracuse (SEAR • ah • kuse) is west of Utica. Syracuse
is one of a string of cities built on the old Erie Canal. At
the Canal Museum in Syracuse you can learn about the
Erie Canal. Machinery, medicines, and dishes are just
three products made in the Syracuse area. The famous
Syracuse University is in the city.

From Syracuse, go through the Finger Lakes. These
lakes really are shaped like fingers—except there are 11
of them!

Above: The Corning Glass Center
Right: Downtown Rochester

Corning is south of the Finger Lakes. Corning is called
the *Crystal City*. Much glass is made there. The mirror
for California's 200-inch Hale telescope was made in
Corning. That is one of the world's biggest telescopes.

From Corning, head back north to Rochester. The city
lies on Lake Ontario. Settlers came here in 1812. The
Erie Canal helped the city grow. Today, Rochester is the
third biggest city in the state.

Left: The Eastman Kodak Company office
Above: The International Museum of Photography
is in the George Eastman House.

Rochester is sometimes called the *Picture City*. That is because more film and cameras are made there than in any other city of the world. Clothes, copying machines, and food products are also made in Rochester.

George Eastman, a Rochester man, invented a simple camera and created new kinds of films. He headed a huge photography company. Eastman's house is now a museum of photography.

From Rochester, head to Buffalo, which is near New York's northwest corner. The city lies on the shores of Lake Erie and is very near Canada. The Holland Land Company formed a settlement here in 1803. Today Buffalo is the state's second biggest city.

Buffalo is our country's leading city for making flour. Iron and steel are also made in Buffalo.

Much history dealing with American presidents has occurred in Buffalo. Millard Fillmore lived in Buffalo before and after he was president. Grover Cleveland was mayor of Buffalo before he became president. In 1901 President William McKinley was shot while in the city. Go to the Wilcox Mansion. This was where Vice-President Theodore Roosevelt became president upon McKinley's death.

You'll enjoy the Museum of Science in Buffalo. You can learn about plants, rocks, and dinosaurs there. You'll also enjoy the art works at the Albright-Knox Art Gallery. If you like sports, you can watch the Buffalo Bills play football or the Buffalo Sabres play hockey.

Left top: The Wilcox Mansion
Left bottom: The Albright-Knox Art Gallery
Above: Red Jacket

Before you leave Buffalo, take a look at the monument to the Indian leader Red Jacket. Red Jacket was a Seneca chief who fought on the English side during the Revolutionary War. But after the war, he tried to keep his people at peace with the Americans. He also worked to preserve his people's culture. Today, there are three Indian reservations near Buffalo. Over 28,000 Indians live in the state. That is one of the higher Indian populations in our country.

Above: The American Falls at Niagara Falls
seen from Prospect Point
Right: A "Cave-of-the-Winds" trip on the
American Falls

Finish your New York trip at Niagara (ni • AG • ah •

rah) Falls, just north of Buffalo. They are the most

famous waterfalls in North America. There are two main

parts to Niagara Falls. The 182-foot-tall American Falls

is in New York. The 171-foot-tall Horseshoe Falls is

across the border in Canada. Every minute, about 400 million pounds of water splashes down Niagara Falls. Some of the water at Niagara Falls is used by power plants to produce electricity.

Places can't tell the whole story of New York. Many interesting people have lived in the Empire State.

Theodore Roosevelt (1858-1919) was born in New York City. As a young man, he worked as a rancher in the Dakota Territory. During the Spanish-American War, he led soldiers known as "Rough Riders." From 1901 to 1909 he served as our 26th president. Theodore Roosevelt also worked hard for peace. He was the first American to win the Nobel peace prize. Did you ever have a "teddy bear"? It was named for Theodore Roosevelt, who was called "Teddy."

Franklin D. Roosevelt's home in Hyde Park

Franklin Delano Roosevelt (1882-1945) was born in Hyde Park. He was a distant cousin of Theodore Roosevelt. Franklin D. Roosevelt was struck by a disease called *polio*. It left his legs crippled. But he didn't give up on what he wanted to do. He was elected governor of New York. Then in 1932 he was elected 32nd president of the United States. "F.D.R." was president for over 12 years—longer than any other person. He helped lead our country through the rough years known as the "Great Depression." He also led us during World War II.

Herman Melville (1819-1891) was born in New York City. While still a teenager, Melville went to sea. He became an author. He wrote novels about the sea. Herman Melville wrote *Moby Dick* and *Billy Budd*.

The Empire State has produced many other great writers. Washington Irving (1783-1859) was born in New York City. He wrote the short stories "Rip Van Winkle" and "The Legend of Sleepy Hollow." Poet Walt Whitman, playwright Eugene O'Neill, and children's author Maurice (maw • REES) Sendak were also born in the state. The great black writer James Baldwin was born in New York City. Baldwin wrote *Nobody Knows My Name* and *Another Country*. Alex Haley, who wrote *Roots*, was born in Ithaca.

Humphrey (HUM • free) Bogart (1899-1957) was born in New York City. He became one of the most famous movie stars of all time. *The Maltese Falcon* and *The African Queen* are just two of his films.

The great baseball player Lou Gehrig (1903-1941) was born in New York City. He holds the record for home runs with the bases loaded: 23. But Gehrig's most famous record is the 2,130 straight games he played in. Boxing champ Gene Tunney, baseball pitchers Whitey Ford and Sandy Koufax, and basketball great Kareem Abdul-Jabbar were born in the Empire State, too.

You remember that Franklin D. Roosevelt had polio. Polio once killed and crippled thousands. Dr. Jonas Salk (SAWK), born in New York City in 1914, found a way to prevent polio. It was named the Salk vaccine.

Anna Mary Robertson Moses (1860-1961) was born on a farm in New York's Washington County. She became an artist when she was 76 years old. "Grandma Moses" was still painting when she was over 100 years old.

A painting by "Grandma Moses"

Lake Champlain is in the northeast corner of New York State.

Shirley Chisholm (CHIZ • um) was born in Brooklyn in 1924. In 1968 Shirley Chisholm was elected to the United States House of Representatives. She became the first black woman to ever serve in our country's Congress.

Home to Theodore Roosevelt . . . Franklin D. Roosevelt . . . Grandma Moses . . . and Shirley Chisholm.

A place where many Revolutionary War battles were fought . . . and where the United Nations now works for peace.

The leading state for making clothes and publishing books . . . and a leader for growing grapes and apples.

A state where you can see Niagara Falls . . .

baseball's Hall of Fame . . . and West Point.

This is New York—the Empire State!

A variety of New York scenes (clockwise from above) are a ski jump at Lake Placid, the United Nations Security Council room, an unusual rock formation called Chimney Bluff, the Chrysler Building in Manhattan, and the Ausable Chasm where you can take a boat ride through the rapids.

Facts About NEW YORK

Area—49,576 square miles (30th biggest state)

Greatest Distance North to South—307 miles

Greatest Distance East to West—314 miles

Boundaries—Lake Ontario, the St. Lawrence River, and Canada to the north; Vermont, Massachusetts, Connecticut, and the Atlantic Ocean to the east; New Jersey and Pennsylvania to the south; Pennsylvania, Lake Erie, the Niagara River, and Canada to the west

Highest Point—5,344 feet above sea level (Mount Marcy)

Lowest Point—Sea level (along the Atlantic Ocean)

Hottest Recorded Temperature—108° (at Troy, on July 22, 1926)

Coldest Recorded Temperature—Minus 52° (at Stillwater Reservoir, on February 9, 1934)

Statehood—Our 11th state, on July 26, 1788

Origin of Name—New York was named in honor of the English Duke of York

Capital—Albany

Counties—62

U.S. Senators—2

U.S. Representatives—34

State Senators—61

State Assemblymen—150

State Motto—*Excelsior* (Latin, meaning "Ever upward")

Nicknames—The Empire State, the Excelsior State (Some think it was George Washington who nicknamed New York the Empire State.)

State Seal—Adopted in 1778

State Flag—Adopted in 1909

State Flower—Rose

State Bird—Bluebird

State Animal—Beaver

State Fish—Brook trout

State Gem—Garnet

State Tree—Sugar Maple

Some Rivers—Hudson, Mohawk, Oswego, Seneca, Susquehanna, Delaware, Genesee, Niagara, St. Lawrence

Some Waterfalls—Niagara, Taughannock, Cohoes, falls at Watkins Glen

Lakes—Over 8,000 (Lake Oneida is the biggest lake that is completely inside the state.)

Some Islands—Long, Manhattan, Staten, Liberty, Ellis, Governors, the Thousand Islands

Some Mountain Ranges—Adirondack, Catskill, Shawangunk

Wildlife—Deer, foxes, beavers, raccoons, black bears, squirrels, minks, muskrats, skunks, pine martens, rabbits, porcupines, woodchucks, wild turkeys, wild ducks, wild geese, pheasants, bluebirds, robins, woodpeckers, many other kinds of birds, frogs, rattlesnakes and other snakes

Fishing—Clams, lobsters, oysters, sea trout, butterfish, striped bass, pike, perch

Farm Products—Milk and milk products, lettuce, celery, cauliflower, cabbage, potatoes, tomatoes, onions, sweet corn, apples, grapes, pears, cherries, strawberries, maple syrup, wine, hay, ducks, chickens, turkeys, eggs

Mining—Salt, oil, zinc, gypsum, clay, talc, garnet

Manufacturing Products—Books and other printed materials, cameras and film, medical and scientific instruments, clothing, food products, chemicals, paper and paper products

Population—1980 census: 17,558,072 (1990 estimate: 18,049,658)

Major Cities	1980 Census	1990 Estimate
New York City	7,071,639	no estimate
Buffalo	357,870	316,675
Rochester	241,741	230,678
Yonkers	195,351	188,720
Syracuse	170,105	160,861
Albany	101,727	94,407

Persons per sq. mi.	Persons per km²
More than 1,000	More than 400
200 to 1,000	77 to 400
50 to 200	20 to 77
Less than 50	Less than 20

ROCHESTER
BUFFALO
SYRACUSE
ALBANY
NEW YORK CITY

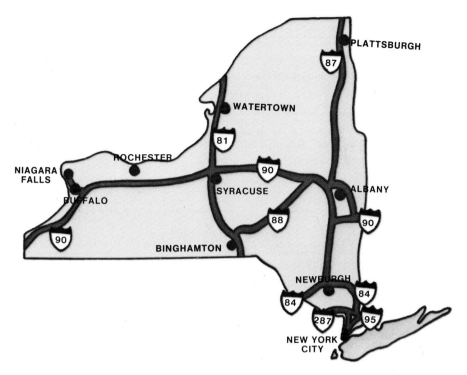

New York History

People first came to New York over 11,000 years ago.

1524—Giovanni da Verrazano, an Italian, may have explored New York Bay
      and the Hudson River in this year

1609—Champlain explores the area for France; in this year Henry
      Hudson explores for The Netherlands

1624—Fort Orange (now Albany) is built by the Dutch

1625—The Dutch start building New Amsterdam (now New York City)

1626—For about $24 worth of goods, the Dutch buy Manhattan Island from
      the Indians

1664—The English take control of New York from the Dutch

1689-1763—During the French and Indian Wars, many battles are fought in
      New York

1754—King's College (now called Columbia University) is founded

1776—During the Revolutionary War, the English take control of New York
      City

1777—The Americans win the Battle of Oriskany as well as the Battle of
      Saratoga

1783—United States wins the Revolutionary War

1785-1789—New York City serves as our nation's capital

1788—On July 26, New York becomes our 11th state

1789—George Washington is inaugurated as our first president on April 30 in
      New York City

1797—Albany becomes the capital of New York

1800—Population of state is 589,051

1802—United States Military Academy opens at West Point

1825—The Erie Canal is completed

1831—New York's first railroad, the Mohawk and Hudson, begins operating

1837-1841—Martin Van Buren, born in Kinderhook, serves as our country's 8th president

1848—Elizabeth Cady Stanton and Lucretia Mott organize our country's first women's rights convention in Seneca Falls

1850-1853—Millard Fillmore, born in Locke, serves as our country's 13th president

1861-1865—New York helps the Union win the Civil War by providing it with the most men and supplies of any state

1879—State Capitol building in Albany opens

1886—Statue of Liberty is dedicated

1894—Present state constitution is adopted

1900—Population of the Empire State reaches 7,268,894

1901—President William McKinley is shot to death in Buffalo; Theodore Roosevelt, born in New York City, become our 26th president and serves until 1909

1917-1918—After the United States enters World War I, New York provides over 518,000 soldiers for the war effort

1918—New York State Barge Canal System opens

Later 1920s-1930s—Great Depression puts many people out of work

1932—Winter Olympics are held at Lake Placid

1933-1945—Franklin Delano Roosevelt, born in Hyde Park, serves as our 32nd president

1939-1940—New York World's Fair is held on Long Island

1941-1945—After the United States enters World War II, 1,638,044 New York men and women are in uniform; the state also produces many war materials

1950—Population of the Empire State reaches 14,830,192

1952—United Nations headquarters are completed in New York City

1964-1965—New York hosts another World's Fair

1967—State creates a lottery to help finance education

1968—Shirley Chisholm, born in Brooklyn, is elected to the U.S. House of Representatives; she becomes the first black woman to serve in our country's Congress

1972—Tropical storm kills 27 and causes great damage in the state

1978—New York Yankees win their 23rd World Series

1980—Winter Olympics are held again at Lake Placid

1983—Mario Cuomo becomes governor

1986—Statue of Liberty centennial celebration is held

1989—David N. Dinkins becomes the first African-American to be elected mayor of New York City

INDEX

INDEX, Cont'd

About the Author:

Dennis Fradin attended Northwestern University on a creative writing scholarship and was graduated in 1967. While still at Northwestern, he published his first stories in *Ingenue* magazine and also won a prize in *Seventeen's* short story competition. A prolific writer, Dennis Fradin has been regularly publishing stories in such diverse places as *The Saturday Evening Post, Scholastic, National Humane Review, Midwest,* and *The Teaching Paper.* He has also scripted several educational films. Since 1970 he has taught second grade reading in a Chicago school—a rewarding job, which, the author says, "provides a captive audience on whom I test my children's stories." Married and the father of three children, Dennis Fradin spends his free time with his family or playing a myriad of sports and games with his childhood chums.

About the Artists:

Len Meents studied painting and drawing at Southern Illinois University and after graduation in 1969 he moved to Chicago. Mr. Meents works full time as a painter and illustrator. He and his wife and child currently make their home in LaGrange, Illinois.

DATE DUE		